Remember Me

Jasmine Williams

BookLeaf Publishing

India | USA | UK

Presentation by *BookLeaf Publishing*

Web: www.bookleafpub.com

E-mail: info@bookleafpub.com

ISBN: 9789357445245

First edition 2021

DEDICATION

I'd like to dedicate this book to everyone in my family, especially my parents and older brother. As well as my best friend, who has read everything I've ever shared and supported me through everything I have faced, and anyone else who considers us close. I love you all

ACKNOWLEDGEMENT

Thank you for taking the time to read this short book. It means the world to me that this book exists, and I hope you enjoy reading it as much as I enjoyed writing it

PREFACE

Everything is poetry~

Starting senior year

Most kids dread going back
But me, I miss the notebook stack.
Homework and essays and writing galore
To me, that stuff just isn't a bore.
I enjoy the hustle of getting to class.
Sitting close to the back to avoid students sass.
I love the sound of pages flipping,
And the frequent noice of backpacks unzipping.
The warmth of freshly printed parchment,
And the shopping for new garment.
I wish I could forever stay this age,
But I know this is just an interstage

Who am I?

Who am I?
I'm the girl in the back row
Who most people don't know exists.
I'm the sixteen year old
Who prefers country music to rap.
I'm the writer
who can't seem to find the confidence to share.
I'm the stranger on the street
Walking with my head down low.
Who am I?
I am a little piece of everyone
But I am nobody in particular.
I am me.
So, who are you?

Red

The beautiful sadness
Of blood,
Dripping from an open wound.
The sky
Just before day turns to night.
A rose with thorns,
Sharp enough to tear through the skin on your
fingertips.
The sweet flavour and aroma
Of fresh strawberries
Straight from the garden.
The colour many describe
As the colour of deep love.
And the colour of the deep scars left
When that love
Suddenly vanishes.

A breath of fresh air

Leave me and see.
I can breathe just fine,
Even on my own.
Perhaps,
I can breath even better
Without you

Love

Let me be the
One you
Volunteer to
Engage with forever

Undefined

Why do we use the word ugly?
To describe that which is not beautiful.
But, who decides
What is beautiful?
That is defined
By the shallow people.
Individuals who don't look beyond
Clear skin,
Small waists,
And muscular builds.
Humans do not need the word.
It is loud and untrue.
Beauty has no definition.
So, why does the word ugly
Exist?

Reincarnation

When I die,
I hope my soul will travel.
I hope it will escape my body
And fly high into the air.
I hope it finds the place
I long to be.
A tall, healthy oak tree,
High on a mountaintop somewhere.
That is where my soul
Will makes its new home.
That is where
It will finally be free

Block

What does a writer do
When they cannot write?
They suffer in the real world,
Struggling to create
Anything they can
From nothing at all.
They try to invoke emotions,
Or madness.
They stir in their own thoughts,
Trying to find the right words.
It's an agonizing process
Of finding your creative light
In an endless tunnel of dark

Selection of the fittest

I'd rather be unseen,
Clinging on cliffs,
Swayed by the breeze of madness
Than to live shunned by everyone
In clusters of
Talented, brilliant souls,
praised and plucked
By ugly human hands.
I'd rather smell of an ancient sea,
Strong and free,
Then to smell of sweet flowers

The future

A thick fog clouds my head.
Fog made of doubt,
Excitement,
And expectations I place on myself.
Fog that burns my eyes
And rips at my throat
As I try to call out.
I can't see through it.
Nor can I tell
If I'm even going the right way.

Anticipation for graduation

A day we all dream of.
Hats, flying through the air.
Soaring up,
Only to fall back down.
Gowns of gold and red,
Partially dragging on the floor
As the grad walks up towards the stage.
Memories flood their minds.
Friends they've met,
Activities they've been part of,
Marks they've made,
And thought of marks they will make.
Looking around,
They realize this is the last time
They will see most of these faces.
They think of where they started,
And how far they have come.
For better
Or worse
They are adults now.
Supposedly ready
to be shoved into Life.

Time travel

If I could go back through time,
There is not a thing I would change.
Because life has been a rocky clime,
And my goals are finally in range.
My past has shaped me this way,
For reasons I'm not yet sure.
So I will stay,
And continue to mature.
Without the help of pain,
Without the help of misery,
There would be no gain,
That is proven through history.

Let it be as it is

In our early years,
We were happy with only
What the land could provide.
We hunted,
We explored,
We did not waste,
Nor kill for fun.
We,
As early humans,
Did not cause
Deforestation
Or animal extinction.
We lived with the land,
Rather than on top of it.
To modern society,
The way humans lived back then,
Was uncivilized and inhuman.
But, what is less humane
Than sending big machines
To rip away land
From small woodland creatures
Who have no defences
Against nasty human technology?
Where is the humanity
In poaching glorious,

Peaceful,
And unexacting animals
For their horns,
Tusks,
Or skins?
How can we say
Humans who killed
Only for the purpose of need and safety,
Were inhuman?
Why is it them
We call uncivil
When we eliminate culture,
Kill each other
With no reason,
Destroy Mother Nature,
And use religion
As a weapon.
We are no more civil
Than the first people
To walk this land.

To my future son

You may stumble,
Fall,
And break.
But you will always get back up.
You may cry,
Scream,
And feel that your fists
Are your only resort.
You will feel alone sometimes,
Desperate and afraid,
But I will be there,
Standing with open arms.
I will cushion your fall,
Hear your screams,
And no matter what,
I will pull you back to your feet
And love you just the same.

Who are you?

I say I want to know you,
And you reply
"No you don't."
But the truth is,
I do.
I want to know
What makes you smile,
And things that make you upset.
I want to know the fears
You don't tell people
Because you don't want to be judged.
The insecurities you hide
Behind a bright smile,
And who broke your heart first.
I want to know
The name of your best friend,
And who your worst enemy is.
Tell me your stories;
Your faults,
Your failures,
your greatest successes,
And most treasured memories.
Tell me why you are
Who you are,
And how hard you fought

To become this person
So I can answer my own question.
Who are you?

Loyalty

I will sit by your side
Through the cold of winter
And the sadness that summer brings.
I will be your shoulder to cry on
And your therapist at two a.m.
Your umbrella in the storm,
And your shield in war.
I won't break your trust,
Even if you break mine.

Homesick

I am homesick.
Not for my house,
Or a person,
But for entire worlds
That I will never see.
Worlds trapped
Between the covers of novels,
And in episodes of animation.
Places where everything is possible
And people outside your world
Don't comment on you
As a person.
A place where everyone belongs
And nobody is ever forgotten

Note to self

Don't worry about the past.
Things you can't change
Need to stay behind you.
Don't plan every second of your future.
You will grow expectations
And will be crushed
If things don't go as planned.
Do not go somewhere
Only to please a friend of yours.
A bad, forced experience
Could ruin other activities.
Don't change who you are
To make temporary friendships.
They will be your greatest downfall.
Live in the moment,
But don't forget that moments
Will always come to an end.
Don't let others determine who you are;
That is a decision that only you
Have the power to make.

Deep in the void

There's a void following us all.
Something that steals from us
Everyday of our lives.
Pens,
Socks,
The left shoe,
And right mitten
That always seems to vanish
From sight.
This void has a way
Of making itself known
Through the tiny inconveniences
That start a horrible day.
Deep in the void
Is where all the lost things
Lay to rest.
Grief,
Pain,
Torment
And despair
Are the feeling that swirl around,
Creating this everlasting void
That hovers around us
And will only expire
When we do.

Please

Let me love you,
And please, love me too.
Like the moon loves the sky,
And birds love to fly.
Accept me as I may be,
And allow me to remain free.
Be gentle like the ocean kissing the shore,
And I beg you, don't close the door.

You saved me today, tomorrow, and forever

I was on the edge,
Tired,
Hopeless,
Alone.
And then you came along.
You cut through the darkness
And emerged
Bright as a spotlight,
Shining down on me.
"You will be found."
You said;
And somehow,
I believed you.
You sang to me to sleep most nights,
Bringing me into your world
And giving me a place
Where I would never disappear.
You held me close
And let your words
Dance through my mind like ripples

on the calm ocean.
Although we are not within arms reach,
The space you hold in my heart
Will never fade.
You will remain with me
For forever